Digital Badges

CHERRY LAKE PUBLISHING • ANN ARBOR, MICHIGAN

by Shauna Masura

CHERRY
LAKE
Publishing

A Note to Adults: Please review the instructions for the activities in this book before allowing children to do them. Be sure to help them with any activities you do not think they can safely complete on their own.

A Note to Kids: Be sure to ask an adult for help with these activities when you need it. Always put your safety first!

Published in the United States of America by Cherry Lake Publishing
Ann Arbor, Michigan
www.cherrylakepublishing.com

Series Editor: Kristin Fontichiaro
Photo Credits: Cover and page 1, Shauna Masura; page 4, ©michaeljung/
Shutterstock, Inc.; page 5, ©Mark Gstohl/www.flickr.com/CC-BY-2.0;
page 6, ©Pink Moose/www.flickr.com/CC-BY-2.0; page 7, ©claudio
zaccherini/Shutterstock, Inc.; page 8, ©wavebreakmedia/Shutterstock, Inc.;
page 9, www.openclipart.org; page 13, ©Kzenon/Shutterstock, Inc.; page 14,
©iofoto/Shutterstock, Inc.; page 17, Kristin Fontichiaro; page 18, ©matka_
Wariatka/Shutterstock, Inc.; page 19, ©jordache/Shutterstock, Inc.; page 21,
©Digital Media Pro/Shutterstock, Inc.; page 22, ©Catalin Petolea/Shutterstock,
Inc.; page 24, ©Morgan Lane Photography/Shutterstock, Inc.; page 27,
©Andresr/Shutterstock, Inc.; pag e 28, ©Ann Baldwin/Shutterstock, Inc.;
page 29, ©Pressmaster/Shutterstock, Inc.

Library of Congress Cataloging-in-Publication Data
Masura, Shauna, author.
  Digital badges/by Shauna Masura.
     pages cm.—(Makers as innovators) (Innovation library)
  Includes bibliographical references and index.
  ISBN 978-1-62431-143-7 (lib. bdg.)—ISBN 978-1-62431-209-0 (e-book)—
ISBN 978-1-62431-275-5 (pbk.)
  1. Rewards and punishments in education—Juvenile literature. 2. Badges—
Juvenile literature. I. Title.
  LB3025.M345 2014
  371.5'3—dc23   2013004806

Cherry Lake Publishing would like to acknowledge the work of The Partnership for
21st Century Skills. Please visit www.p21.org for more information.

Printed in the United States of America
Corporate Graphics Inc.
July 2013
CLFA13

21st Century Skills INNOVATION LIBRARY

Contents

Chapter 1

Show What You've Done

Wherever you go in life, you will always be learning. So will the people around you. Some things, such as multiplication and writing essays, we learn in school. Some

Your report card doesn't show the important things you do outside of school.

SUBJECT	1st	Period 2nd	3rd	Term Exam.	Term Av.	1st	Period 2nd	3rd	Term Exam.	Term Av.	Yrly. Av.
Homemaking II	A	A	A		A	A	A	A-		A-	A-
Typ. 1	A+	A	A+		A+	A+	A+	A+	A		A+
P. Geom.	A	A-	A-		a-	B+	a-	B-		B+	
Eng. III	A	A-	A		a	a-	A	A		a-	
Conduct	A	B+	a-			B+	B+	B+			
Days Absent	—	2	4			2	—	—			
Times Tardy	—	—	—			—	—	—			

NAME Tigert, Ann AGE 16 GRADE 11 YEAR 1949

........................, Teacher

Report cards are a good way to see how well you are doing in your classes.

things, such as learning to drive, we learn in the community. And still more things—such as lawn mowing or cooking—we learn at home. Learning doesn't always mean you are sitting in a classroom. We learn everywhere, throughout our lives.

At the end of every school year, you get a report card from your teachers. It shows all the subjects you studied and how well you performed in each one. It's how schools communicate your progress to you, your parents, and your future teachers. But does this tell everything about you? No! You know a lot more cool stuff than what appears on a report card, right? A report card doesn't show what a good babysitter you are. It doesn't show the

Many clubs and organizations award badges to their members.

cool skateboarding trick you just learned or that you were able to knit a scarf for your grandmother's birthday. Where do those skills get recorded?

When scouts learn new skills or complete projects, they earn merit **badges** and patches. Look at the photo above. What do you think these badges represent? We can see the scout's troop number and that he or she went to space camp. We can also see a badge with books on it. This one might tell us that the scout likes to read. From just these few clues, we can start to understand who this scout is and what he or she is able to do.

Report cards and scout badges are just two ways to show what we know. For years, people have been coming up with other ways to show their out-of-school achievements. Varsity letters indicate athletic skills. Passport stamps and bumper stickers show where you've traveled. Sticker charts show how often chores are completed.

Each of these symbols marks an accomplishment that you should be proud of, but many times the

As people travel around the world, their passports get filled with stamps from different countries.

knowledge and skills that go along with out-of-school experiences go unnoticed. Wouldn't it be great if you could showcase all the things you have done in the same way? And wouldn't it be cool if all of your accomplishments could be put together in one place?

You're not the only person asking this question. Lots of game designers, teachers, and hobbyists have been wondering the same thing. Even big organizations want to get involved. Some computer programmers have taken the badges that scouts have used for years and put them on the Internet. They call it digital badging.

What's Missing from Your Report Card?

You are more than the grades on your report card. With digital badges, you have a way to show that to the world! If you could add one thing to your report card, what would it be? What do you want people to know about you?

Chapter 2

What Are Badges?

A digital badge is an online image that tells people about a new skill that you've learned. Take a look at the running badge on this page. How much can you learn just by looking at it? Probably not very much. Digital badges are cool because they also have **metadata**. Metadata is information that is built into a digital object. Digital badges have a lot of metadata packed inside of them. Clicking a badge will show you

Digital badges are usually accompanied by graphics that show what the collector did to earn them.

- who gave out the badge (the **issuer**);
- who earned the badge (the **collector**);

- when the collector earned the badge;
- the activities the collector had to do to earn the badge (the **criteria**); and
- in many cases, a video or photograph of the project the collector completed to earn the badge (the **evidence**).

Check out the description on this running badge. Notice how you can see the criteria for earning the badge. It even points you to specific evidence to prove that each badge collector finished the race. You can also see the badge issuer and when the badge was created.

Open Badges

Digital badges have become an important tool for learners everywhere. This is largely thanks to the system of Open Badges, pioneered by the Mozilla Foundation. Mozilla is an organization that creates and maintains software for anyone to use online. It sets the standards for creating digital badges and made the whole system open to the global community of learners. Thanks to Mozilla, anyone can earn a badge and share it with others. Check out *http://openbadges.org* to learn more about what Mozilla continues to add to the digital badge movement.

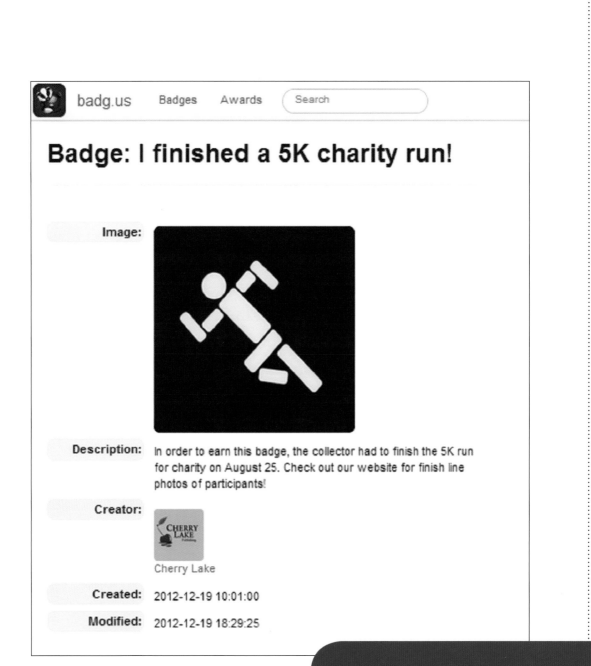

badg.us   Badges   Awards   (Search)

Badge: I finished a 5K charity run!

Image:

Description: In order to earn this badge, the collector had to finish the 5K run for charity on August 25. Check out our website for finish line photos of participants!

Creator:

CHERRY LAKE

Cherry Lake

Created: 2012-12-19 10:01:00

Modified: 2012-12-19 18:29:25

Finishing a charity run is just one example of an accomplishment worthy of a badge.

Chapter 3

Earning Badges and Meeting Challenges

Badges are given out only when you accomplish something new or important. Everyday things that you already do, like completing your homework or brushing your teeth, aren't going to earn you a badge. Let's face it. How exciting would it be to show friends your toothbrushing badge anyway? When you try to earn a badge, you are learning or doing something that will help you stretch and grow in new ways.

When individuals or organizations issue a badge, they are sending out a challenge. It is a way of saying, "This is something we know how to do. Why don't you try it?"

Look at the badge from chapter 2. It's pretty obvious what you need to do to earn it. That's a good example of a badge that is issued because you've completed a task or demonstrated a skill.

Badges can also be given for what people call soft skills. Soft skills are behaviors or attitudes such as

Being helpful around the house is one way that you can show your soft skills.

helpfulness or perseverance. We can't always measure soft skill achievements with a photograph. These kinds of skills tend to be observed or noticed by someone. They're a really important part of being a good community member. They're also a really important part of what makes you you! We don't pick our friends

Think about how hard you work at school. Wouldn't it be great if there was a way that teachers could recognize your effort?

solely by what they do. We choose them because we like their sense of humor, their kindness, and their generosity. Badging helps us celebrate those traits in ourselves and in others.

So what about the badge on the opposite page? How could you learn more about the kind of behaviors you would need to demonstrate to earn a badge for

Some badges are designed to reward people for showing good character rather than completing tasks.

leadership? In this example, you must help organize a service project at school. To complete this challenge, you might need to brainstorm ways to help people in your community. You might meet with teachers to plan for the day or coordinate events for your classmates. Once you know what the badge issuer is looking for, it's time to put it into action and demonstrate your leadership to others.

How do you show that with evidence? You could supply a certificate of attendance, a video of you working with younger kids, or a letter from your teacher. You might use a single piece of evidence or a collection of smaller pieces of evidence. Just check the badge criteria to match what the issuer is looking for.

If you want to earn a badge but you get stuck, ask the badge issuer for help. When someone issues a badge challenge, they're also offering to support you as you work toward the goal. You're never alone when you're learning in life! Counselors, teachers, parents, classmates, coaches, and religious leaders are all people who help us learn. They can't do the work for you, but they have the **expertise** to help you get where you're going.

Guess what? Maybe you haven't tried to earn a badge, but someone you know has noticed your leadership. He or she might surprise you with a badge nomination!

Badge Collectors in Action

This student is a badge collector who participates in an after-school club that issues badges. Her mentors challenged her to use conductive dough and her knowledge of electronic circuitry to create a pig with lights for eyes and a rotating tail. She worked with her classmates to complete the project. When they were successful, their mentors gave them a sticker with a picture of a digital badge and a claim code. When she goes home, she can go online to claim the badge and put it in her badge backpack.

Chapter 4

Issuing Badges

Do you like gardening? Create a badge for people who grow flowers.

Earning badges is a lot of fun! But being part of a community means you also have a responsibility to share. How about issuing a badge challenge for someone else?

It is important for badge issuers to provide support as collectors work toward their goal. The first thing you need when providing support is expertise. You need some experience doing what you are challenging others to do. If you've never skateboarded before, then you're probably not the best person to give out skateboarding badges. You won't be able to coach collectors on good techniques, and you won't know when they've done something well.

You Are an Expert!

Believe it or not, you have expertise, and you can issue a badge challenge to others! Try brainstorming a list of things you're good at. If you're struggling to think of something, ask your friends and family what they think you do well. You can also try these questions:

- What do you do for fun?
- What are your hobbies?
- What do you and your friends do when you're hanging out?

Be specific as you write up the instructions for your badge. When a collector says that he got an A in science, you might congratulate him for a job well done, but you don't know exactly what he did to achieve that grade. You can't see the evidence. Maybe he had one big test that counted for the entire grade. Maybe the grade came from a couple big projects the whole year. Maybe he was able to revise his work multiple times before the teacher gave a final grade. It is impossible to tell what skills were developed when you see only a letter grade.

Carefully consider the instructions you create for your badges.

As an issuer, you need to decide how you want your badge earners to collect and display their work online. You also need to provide a Web address that will direct people to a site where they can view the evidence that is tied to the badge.

Here are some easy, low-tech ways that you can collect evidence for the badges that you issue:

- Create a wiki where badge earners can add their evidence. This option allows people completing the badge challenge to interact by commenting, editing, and adding to collaborative work.
- Use an online form to collect evidence, and post a spreadsheet so others can see. This option allows issuers a bit more control over the kinds of evidence that they want collectors to provide.
- Have collectors upload photos of their work online. Add the photos to a shared, public photo gallery.

If you like to go camping, you might create badges for setting up a tent or starting a fire.

Now you're ready to create your badge. First, you'll need an image. You can draw it on your computer, take a photo, or use a Creative Commons image (use *http://search.creativecommons.org* to find images that people have given permission for others to use).

The image you select should represent something about the skill. For example, a photo of a tent works well for a camping badge. Next, you'll need to use a badge generator Web site. That's a site that will take your image, your criteria, and all of the other metadata and **bake** it together into a digital badge. In this book, we've used Badg.us (*http://badg.us*) because it's free and open to all. Work with your parents to create a shared account if you are less than 13 years old.

Once your badge is hosted online, it's time to invite people to your challenge. You can e-mail your friends, put up a poster at school, or talk about your badge during morning announcements.

As people work on the challenge, there's one tricky part for you. When you issue a badge, you're putting your reputation on the line. You're saying, "These people did what the badge says they did." Before you put your stamp of approval on someone's work, carefully check that he or she has really earned it. Follow the instructions in your badge generator to issue the badge and congratulate the collector for the achievement!

Chapter 5

Displaying Badges

O nce you've earned a couple of badges, you'll
want to show them off. One of the fun things
about collecting digital badges is finding
places to display your accomplishments online.
A lot of badges can be posted on blogs or Web
pages. Just keep your privacy in mind. Whenever you
post something on the Internet, it can be viewed by
anyone—your friends, your teachers, your parents,
and even total strangers. So be safe online. For
example, do not include your last name or other
personal details.

You might collect badges from several different
badge generators. How do you put them all together
in one place? You need a digital backpack. The Mozilla
Foundation, a **not-for-profit** organization that creates
and maintains software for anyone to use online, has
created a digital backpack system. Its backpack helps
collectors put all of their badges in a single place. It

Ask a parent or teacher for help if you aren't sure whether you should post something online.

doesn't matter where the badges were earned. You can move your badges from badge generator sites into your Mozilla backpack. From there, you can group your badges in different ways and share those groupings with other people.

Badges, like most things that are published online, leave lasting digital footprints. Right now, you probably aren't looking for a job or applying to college, but someday you might be. It is important to remember that the badges you collect and display should present you in the best possible light.

Grouping Your Badges

Just like a real backpack, your digital backpack can hold a lot of stuff. Once you get your badge backpack up and running, you can organize your badges into different groups or categories. This is helpful because you might want to show off different badges to your friends than you would show off to your teachers. Organizing your badges into different groups can also be a fun way to reflect on all your accomplishments and think about areas where there is room for you to learn more.

When people view your badges, they can learn more about your skills and behaviors. They might become inspired to seek out new learning opportunities and grow their knowledge and skills. They can see

Your friends and family will be impressed as you collect more and more badges.

the path that you took and model their own experiences on what you have done. In that sense, displaying badges helps you be a role model for others. Widgets can help you display your badge backpack contents on the Web. Check out *www.cherrylakepublishing.com/links* for samples you can try.

The digital badging movement opens up new ways for us to express ourselves and tell our stories to others. Your story may just be beginning. You'll continue to grow, change, and learn new things for your entire life. Badges can help you seek out new opportunities and recognize your own accomplishments. Happy badging!

Glossary

badges (BAJ-uz) pins, cloth patches, or digital images that represent something you have learned

bake (BAYK) a slang term for the process of combining an image and metadata to become a digital badge

collector (kuh-LEK-tur) someone who earns and collects digital badges

criteria (krye-TEER-ee-uh) the steps and processes a badge collector needs to complete to earn a badge

evidence (EV-uh-dents) information or facts that help prove something is true or not true

expertise (ek-spur-TEEZ) the skills and abilities of an expert

issuer (ISH-oo-ur) someone who creates and offers a badge challenge and awards the badges

metadata (MEH-tuh-day-tuh) information about a badge challenge that is attached to a digital badge

not-for-profit (NAHT FORE PRAH-fit) meant to benefit society instead of making money

Find Out More

BOOKS

Attwood, Philip. *Acquisitions of Badges (1978–1982)*. London: British Museum, 1985.

Boy Scouts of America. *2012 Boy Scout Requirements*. Irving, TX: Boy Scouts of America, 2012.

Girl Scouts of the United States of America. *Girl Scout Badges and Signs*. New York: Girl Scouts of the U.S.A., 1990.

WEB SITES

Badg.us
http://badg.us
Badg.us is an open-source badge-generating site. If you're under age 13, ask your parents if you can share their account.

Mozilla Open Badge Infrastructure
http://openbadges.org
On this site, you can gather badges from many badge issuers and display them together. If you're under age 13, ask your parents if you can share their account.

Index

About the Author

Shauna Masura is a librarian from Rolling Meadows, Illinois, and the author of *Record It! Shooting and Editing Digital Video*, for Cherry Lake Publishing. She is very excited about the possibilities for digital badging and can't wait to help students get involved in the movement!